A CENTURY OF PRESTON BUS ROUTES

MIKE RHODES

AMBERLEY

First published 2022

Amberley Publishing
The Hill, Stroud
Gloucestershire, GL5 4EP

www.amberley-books.com

Copyright © Mike Rhodes, 2022

The right of Mike Rhodes to be identified as
the Author of this work has been asserted in
accordance with the Copyrights, Designs and
Patents Act 1988.

ISBN 978 1 3981 0878 3 (print)
ISBN 978 1 3981 0879 0 (ebook)

British Library Cataloguing in Publication Data.
A catalogue record for this book is available from
the British Library.

Origination by Amberley Publishing.
Printed in the UK.

Introduction

From 1904 until 1922 the town's public transport system had been solely provided by the Corporation's electric trams. These had commenced running in June 1904 with services radiating out from the town centre to the districts of Broadgate (Penwortham), Ashton, Fulwood, Deepdale, Ribbleton and Farringdon Park. Residents in the Frenchwood and Adelphi/Plungington areas of the town had for many years lobbied the town council for the provision of their own tramway services. However, a service to the latter could not be resolved, due mainly to the principal thoroughfares being too narrow to support an electric tramway. Nevertheless, the residents continued to make protestations and eventually the council agreed to provide a service with motorbuses. Three of Leyland Motor's thirty-seat G7 model, fitted with English Electric bodies, were purchased to operate the service, which duly commenced running on Monday 23 January 1922. Starting in Birley Street, alongside the Town Hall, it ran via Friargate, Fylde Street, Fylde Road, Brook Street and Lytham Road, where it terminated at the junction of Black Bull Lane. It then returned to town via Plungington Road, Adelphi Street, Friargate, Cheapside and Fishergate to Birley Street. In November of that year the route was altered to run out and back via Adelphi Street and Plungington Road.

It was to be 1924 before any further bus routes were inaugurated. From Thursday 5 June the upper part of Frenchwood finally got its bus route and again this commenced as a circular route running anticlockwise from the Town Hall via Lancaster Road, Church Street, Manchester Road, Ruskin Street, Bence Road, Brixton Road, Moore Street and London Road and back to the town centre. It also operated in the reverse direction via the same roads. The route was extended to Ashworth Grove at lower Frenchwood and altered to run out and back via Manchester Road in February 1929. Also, in June 1924, an additional bus service was provided that started from Corporation Street (buses showed Central Station) and ran to Ashton Lane Ends. This was the first of a number of routes that specifically served the Lane Ends area of Ashton over the following fifty-six years. In May 1925, a fourth bus service commenced running, which ran from the cemetery at Farringdon Park to Ashton Lane Ends, on Sunday afternoons only. It was primarily intended as a leisure service to Haslam Park and operated along the arterial road (now known as Blackpool Road). This had been made possible by the opening of Oxheys Bridge, which spanned the Preston to Carlisle railway, in December 1923. A weekday service was introduced in September 1932 between the same two destinations but was routed via a series of back roads to serve a number of cotton mills in the Tulketh and Ashton districts. The last remnant of the service wasn't withdrawn until December 1999.

Between July 1932 and December 1935, the electric tram services were converted to operation by motorbuses. Also, throughout the 1930s the Lytham Road service was successively extended to Boys Lane and then Queens Drive. Two additional services to Ashton Lane Ends also commenced running and the new pre-war housing estates at Holme Slack and Moorside (Moor Nook) gained their first bus routes. Additionally, a service to Gamull Lane via North Road, St Paul's Road, Deepdale Road and Watling Street Road, with a handful of journeys extended to

Longsands Lane, also commenced running in 1937. The period during the Second World War was not unnaturally devoid of any further expansion of the route network and wartime restrictions were applied with some routes suspended and operating times curtailed. Consequently, the next route alterations were not implemented until November 1946 when the Ashton services were revised. In 1947 a service to Trafford Street (Plungington) using two of under-employed Leyland Lions was trialled but this was short-lived.

Significant alterations to the town's route network took place on 1 January 1948 with the implementation of a joint service agreement with Ribble and Scout Motors. A new series of 'P' prefixed routes commenced running to destinations outside of the borough boundary. Buses were provided by both the Corporation and Ribble. Surprisingly the 'P' group of routes remained largely unaltered for nearly twenty years, with only three additional routes being added in the mid-1960s to 1970s. During the 1950s the service to Moor Nook (formerly Moorside) was extended and towards the end of the decade the new housing estate at Brookfield gained its first bus services.

Two peculiarities of the Corporation's services during the 1950s/1960s was the implementation of a reduced timetable on Thursday afternoons, this being half-day closing, and the extension/ deviation of some inbound early morning buses on a number of routes to operate via the railway station. The 1960s was a quiet period for service alterations other than the introduction of the department's first one-person operated (OPO) buses on a number of routes, in December 1968, and the transfer of all services to the new bus station on 12 October 1969. Similarly, the 1970s produced very little change to the network other than new services to the Callon and Grange estates, which were provided by new thirty-one-seat, Duple-bodied Bristol LHS buses – this being the department's first deviation from buses of Leyland manufacture. In April 1978 through running of the P5 between Ribbleton and Hutton and the P2 between Fulwood and Penwortham ceased, with Borough of Preston solely operating the sections of route within the borough. Finally, the PL service was further extended, in August 1978, to the newly commissioned Royal Preston Hospital.

Route letters for the bus routes were first introduced around 1930, and this method of service identification remained in use until 3 November 1980 when route numbers were used for the first time. The full list of letters used over the intervening years is shown on the next page. Of some significance with the introduction of route numbers was the provision of a new service to Tanterton, which was achieved by extending the former Lane Ends service, and the alteration of the service to Lea to run via Garstang Road. Subsequent route numbers used to the present day are far too numerous to list in a similar fashion.

Various alterations to existing services took place during the 1980s, but no new services were introduced until April 1987 when, as a consequence of bus deregulation, there followed a prolonged period of intense competition between Preston Bus, Ribble and newcomer United Transport (t/a Zippy). In addition, there were also a number of other bus operators to contend with. Prior to deregulation the only localities served outside of the borough and the adjoining council districts had been Hutton and Penwortham with the jointly operated P5 and P2 services respectively. In response to competition a whole host of new destinations were served, which included Bamber Bridge, Blackpool, Broughton, Longton, Lytham St Annes, Penwortham, Southport and Woodplumpton, although many of these were short-lived ventures. The period of change prior to and after deregulation has been covered in much more detail in a companion volume penned by the same author. By the end of 1989 some calm had descended on proceeding; indeed, the 1990s proved to be another quiet period, with the only notable event being the provision of the first bus services (albeit only at peak times) to the fledgling developing area of Cottam, to the north of the borough. These services would be further developed throughout the first two decades of the twentieth century.

A*/24	Pedders Lane Ashton	LS/36/6	Longsands Lane
A	Ashton (Lane Ends)	M	Moorside
B	Ashton Inkerman Street	M	Moor Nook
B	Ashton (Lane Ends)	MN/7/8	Moor Nook
BF/36/6	Brookfield via Deepdale	O#	Other Service
BR*/21	Broadgate	P*	Penwortham (see Broadgate)
C/LEC	Cemetery and Lane Ends	PL	Lytham Road
C	Lane Ends Ashton	PL	Boys Lane
CL	Callon Estate	PL	Queens Drive
CR/35/5	Brookfield via Cromwell Road	PL/22/23	Fulwood via Plungington Road
D	Ashton Lane Ends	R*	Ribbleton Chatburn Road
D*/15	Fulwood via Deepdale (Inner Circle)	TS	Trafford Street
F*/20	Fulwood via North Rd (Outer Circle)	P1	Frenchwood to Lea
FP**/16	Farringdon Park	P1	Frenchwood to Larches Estate
FR	Frenchwood	P2	Lightfoot Lane to Penwortham
FR/37/7	Fulwood Row via Deepdale	P3	Frenchwood to Lea
G/12	Grange Estate via Moor Nook	P4	Lightfoot Lane to Penwortham
GL	Gamull Lane or Longsands Lane	P4/34/44	Ingol
GL/10/11	Ribbleton Gamull Lane	P5	Hutton Anchor Inn to Ribbleton
HPC/98	Cemetery and Lane Ends	P6/43	Ingol Redcar Avenue
HS/14	Holme Slack	P7/30/31	Savick Estate

* Originally electric tram routes ** originally a horse tram/electric tram route
# displayed on special services such as Football, Schools and Works

The company had been privatised with an employee/management buyout in 1993 and continued to thrive until Stagecoach Ribble mounted an aggressive expansion policy in the summer of 2007, which resulted in a buyout of Preston Bus in January 2009. Prior to this the revolutionary Orbit circular routes had been implemented in October 2006. What happened over the following two years has been well documented, concluding with the company being sold on to Rotala plc in January 2011. Prior to and during the Stagecoach period of operation many route changes took place, most of which had to be reversed. Rotala acquired the business with a set pattern of routes that served most of the city environs, while Stagecoach retained the routes to Grange, Moor Nook and Ribbleton. The first decade of Rotala's tenure proved to be extremely eventful with many county council-supported services being operated throughout the Fylde and East/West Lancashire. During this period additional centres of population served by Rotala Preston Bus included Appley Bridge, Barnoldswick, Barton, Blackburn, Burscough, Chipping, Chorley, Clitheroe, Croston, Eccleston, Fleetwood, Gisburn, Goosnargh, Great Eccleston, Kirkham, Leyland, Longridge, Mellor, Myerscough, Ormskirk, Parbold, Poulton-le-Fylde, Ribchester, Skelmersdale, Skipton, Thornton-Cleveleys, Whalley, Wrightington and Wigan. A representation of some of these routes has been included, but the limitation of space prevents a full coverage of all the services. The majority of the contract services passed to other operators in the closing years of the decade.

The majority of bus services originally departed from on-street bus stands located in Birley Street, Church Street/Fishergate, Jacson Street and Lancaster Road. The exceptions were the A and B services to Ashton Lane Ends, which departed from Corporation Street until May 1954, and the jointly operated P4 service to Ingol, which departed from a stand on the Express Coach station. Town/City services that have used on-street bus stands in more recent times have been the Park & Ride services (Fishergate/Lune Street & Jacson Street) and services 89 to Larches and 12 to Longton, which have both used the same stand in Lune Street. Four temporary bus stations – situated at Corporation Street, Queen Street, Ribbleton Lane/Fletcher Road and St Peter's Square – were used during Guild week in 1972 while Bow Lane performed a similar function during the 1992 Guild.

The last section of this book touches on the variety of other services that have been operated over the years. These comprise Baths Specials, Excursions & Tours, Events Specials, Football Specials, Hospital Services, Leisure Services, Park & Ride Services, Private Hires, Rail Replacements, School Buses, Shoppers Services and Works Services. Of special note in the aforementioned list are the Baths, Football, Hospital and Works services. The former commenced running in 1938 with the objective of transporting primary school children to Saul Street Baths in Lancaster Road. When the baths closed in 1991 transport continued to be provided to both Fulwood and West View leisure centres until 2015 when Preston Bus relinquished the contract. Football Specials first operated with trams in the early 1900s, but in 1938 a comprehensive network of bus services was provided that ran on match days from many parts of the town and employed as many as twenty buses. These dwindled during the 1960s, but two services were reintroduced for the 2021/2022 season, having been suspended since March 2020 as a result of the Coronavirus pandemic. Dedicated service buses were provided to Sharoe Green Hospital (1952–81) and the Continuation Hospital in Fulwood (1951–84) at specific visiting times. Finally, the cotton mills and engineering complex at Strand Road of Dick, Kerr/English Electric/BAC generated a large number of special buses for several decades during and after the Second World War.

It has not been possible within the constraints of this publication to produce a full history of route developments over the last 100 years, although the author does have comprehensive details of all route changes and developments that have taken place. Some of the pictures are from the author's collection and are indicated as 'MRC' where the original photographer is not known.

Mike Rhodes, January 2022

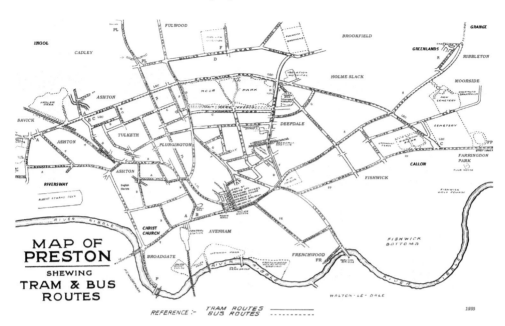

Although produced in different styles, these two diagrams show the extent of the Corporation bus routes operated in 1935 (above) and those operated by Rotala Preston Bus (below) at the start of 2021. At the beginning of 1935 the Fulwood Circulars (converted to buses in December) were still operated by trams and the most northerly and westerly that buses reached were Boys Lane and Pedders Lane respectively (some additional information has been added by the author). The map below shows the extent to which services had penetrated in these directions. There is, however, one or two inaccuracies in that the 14 at Longsands had been replaced by the 49 (in July 2020) and cut back to the original Holme Slack terminus. Some routes, which extend beyond the borough boundary, are not shown in full.

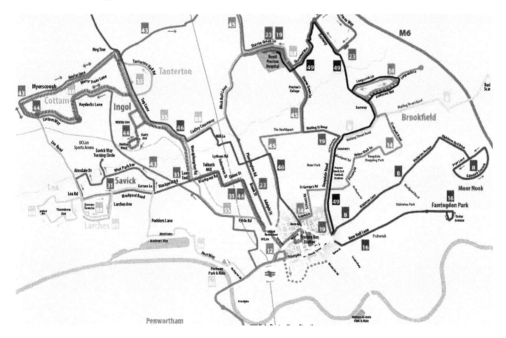

Ashton

Ashton-on-Ribble was first connected to the town centre by a horse-drawn tramway, which commenced running on 23 December 1882. This was replaced by an electric tram service from 30 June 1904, which had a different routing in the Ashton area. The trams were replaced by new English Electric-bodied lowbridge Leyland TD3c buses on 6 August 1934. The route letter used was A, which duplicated the letter used for the Ashton Lane Ends service. Nos 6 and 9 are seen alongside St Peter's Church in Fylde Road where the navvies are engaged in taking up the tram tracks and laying new granite setts. (MRC)

Low-height trams and lowbridge buses were required to operate the A (main-line) service owing to the restricted headroom under the railway bridge in Fylde Road. The TD3cs were largely replaced by eight PD1As and four PD2/10s between 1947 and 1954. The bridge is just visible in the distance of this view of one of the PD1As, from the batch Nos 103–7, which is depicted drifting down an almost deserted Fylde Road on 4 March 1955. The road level under the bridge was lowered in 1957, thus eliminating the need for specific low-height buses. (MRC)

The electric tram service had departed from Harris Street, but the replacement bus service used a stand in Jacson Street. Post-war, the departure point was first moved back to Harris Street and finally to Birley Street. The distinctive bus shelters were first erected in January 1949. MCCW-bodied Leyland PD3/5 No. 66 is seen on the stand in the mid-1960s. Adjacent is the Grade I listed Harris Museum and Art Gallery/Library. (MRC)

The open-air market is in full swing in this spring 1967 view. In January 1967 the HS and A stands were swapped round, and Leyland PD2/10 No. 44 is seen just pulling off the reallocated stand. No. 44 itself was only outshopped in the new blue and ivory colours in January of that year. At this time services A, C and PL followed the same route out of town via Fishergate and Lune Street (Fox Street from March 1968) to Friargate. (MRC/Roy Marshall)

Whereas the trams had followed a route to the top of Tulketh Road (extended via Long Lane to Waterloo Road until 1922), the replacement bus service turned left at Long Lane (now Blackpool Road) where the terminus was located. It then returned via Pedders Lane and Egerton Road to Tulketh Road. OPO buses were introduced to the service on 6 May 1971 (M-Sa) and 5 September 1976 (Su) and the service was renumbered to 24 in November 1980. Seddon-bodied Leyland Panther No. 235 was recorded in Pedders Lane, opposite Ashton Park, on 17 July 1981.

Service 24 continued to run until 25 June 1984 when it was replaced by new service 25, which followed the same route as the 24 to Pedders Lane but then continued on to Aldfield Avenue at Lea. ELC-bodied Atlantean No. 164 is seen in Water Lane on 29 August 1983, not long after road-widening works had been completed. The bold letters of 'ENGLISH ELECTRIC' can be seen in the background.

Following the success of the Lytham Road service two further bus services were introduced in June 1924, running from the town centre to Frenchwood and Corporation Street to Ashton Lane Ends. The latter was later given the route letter A. In August 1934 service B commenced running from Corporation Street to Lane Ends via a different route and the buses then swapped routes at the Lane Ends terminus. Leyland-bodied Tiger No. 73 is seen at the top of Corporation Street sometime between 2 November 1936 and 25 March 1937 when the B service was curtailed at Haslam Park due to bridge works. (MRC)

The original service B was re-lettered to D and rerouted in November 1946. At the same time service A was also re-lettered to B, which then operated by a somewhat different route in the Ashton area. The starting point was moved from Corporation Street to Harris Street in May 1954. Leyland PD1A No. 73 is seen in Corporation Street, heading for the town centre, in this 1958 view. The last day of operation was 12 February 1965. From May 1951 until its cessation the Ashton terminus had been in Inkerman Street. (MRC)

The Ashton Lane Ends C commenced running on 13 November 1936. It initially started from a stand in Jacson Street but was moved to Harris Street in April 1947. It was linked with the Holme Slack HS service in October 1943, a practice that continued until December 1972. Originally new in 1933, Leyland TD3 No. 56 was one of four pre-war Titans to be rebodied by Crofts of Glasgow in 1945. It is seen in Harris Street waiting to leave for Lane Ends in the mid-1950s. (MRC)

The Lane Ends C departed from Bay 26 at the new bus station for the remainder of its existence. This 1970 view depicts Crossley-bodied Leyland PD2/10 No. 30 arriving back at the bus station. No. 30 was one of the last buses to remain in service in maroon and cream and was withdrawn in September of that year. (MRC)

The Lane Ends terminus was moved from Blackpool Road (previously Addison Road) to Kimberley Road in November 1952. The route was converted to OPO, deploying Leyland Panthers on 1 December 1972 (M-Sa) and 5 September 1976 (Su). Marshall-bodied Leyland Panther No. 216 was caught in a downpour at the terminus on 8 September 1977, under the arch of a rainbow.

A fourth bus route commenced running from the cemetery to Ashton Lane Ends (via the Arterial Road) on Sunday afternoons only from 10 May 1925. This later used the letter C and then LEC. It was withdrawn in December 1956. From 19 September 1932 an additional service, referred to by the letters HPC, connected the same two points but ran via a series of back roads. This route later took the letters LEC but usually the letter O (Other) was displayed. MCCW-bodied Leyland PD3A/1 No. 85 is about to emerge from Ripon Street on 1 June 1979. By then a single journey, the service was discontinued after 31 December 1999.

A horse-drawn tram service to the bottom of Fishergate Hill commenced running on 3 June 1882. This was replaced by an electric tram service, which served the full length of Broadgate, on 30 June 1904. Later, the route letter P (Penwortham) was adopted. Along with the linked FP service buses replaced trams on 4 July 1932. Not long afterwards the route was re-lettered to BR and the service was linked with the MN in August 1953. This mid-1950s view depicts Alexander-bodied Leyland PD1 No. 85 alongside Miller Arcade, on the Birley Street stand. (MRC)

The route was one of the first to be converted to OPO on 2 December 1968. Through running to Moor Nook was discontinued, and the route was linked with the Brookfield services. From 3 November 1980 the route number 21 was adopted. Alexander-bodied Atlantean No. 144 was photographed turning at the end of Broadgate on 19 February 1983. St Walburge's Church steeple is prominent on the horizon.

The 21 was converted to operation by minibuses from 19 July 1987 (SuO but withdrawn in October) and 11 April 1988 (M-Sa), with buses running in a loop via South Meadow Lane and Wolseley Road. The service was withdrawn in the 1990s before being reintroduced on 22 April 2002, only to be withdrawn again in July 2007, after which it was operated by Blue Bus of Horwich and then Stagecoach. MCW Metrorider No. 10 was photographed turning from South Meadow Lane into Wolseley Road on 13 April 1995.

From 2 November 2009 services 3A/B (Penwortham/Longton) were rerouted to serve Broadgate in lieu of the 21, but the latter briefly reappeared in May/June 2011 as a temporary service. From July 2012 the 3A was altered to terminate at Broadgate while new services 12A/13A (Longton/Penwortham) also served the district. The 3A was dropped in June 2013, while service 13 replaced the 12A/13A from 4 April 2016. Optare Solo No. 20778 is seen on a diverted 3A in Hartington Road on 3 September 2012.

The final chapter to date regarding bus services in the Broadgate area goes back to 4 April 2016 when first the second and then the third incarnation of service 114 (which had previously served Frenchwood) was rerouted between Preston and Whittle-le-Woods and diverted to serve Broadgate, thus replacing the 12A and 13A. However, this county council contract service was reawarded to Holmeswood Coaches in July 2020. Optare Solo No. 20777 is seen in Wolseley Road on 18 December 2017.

Brookfield

Brookfield was one of a number of post-war housing estates that sprang up in the 1950s/1960s. The first service to the area was the original Gamull Lane GL service, which was introduced on 15 April 1937 and turned around at the then country outpost of the junction of Watling Street Road and Fulwood Row. This then became the FR (previously used for the Frenchwood service) on 1 January 1948. The Brookfield BF was introduced on 24 July 1958 and was routed via Deepdale Road, terminating at a new turning circle at the junction of Watling Street Road and Croasdale Avenue. MCCW-bodied Leyland PD3A/1 No. 72 is seen passing North End's 'old' Deepdale ground on 26 August 1976.

Another variation to Brookfield was the CR, which was routed via Ribbleton Lane/Avenue and Cromwell Road. The initial service, which commenced running on 8 March 1952, was a circular that ran on Saturdays only. In August 1953 it was extended from Dunsop Road to Croasdale Avenue as an out-and-back service. The following year a daily timetable was introduced with an extension to Fulwood Row, which lasted until July 1958 when the terminus reverted back to Croasdale Avenue. Over a period of time the CR/FR had been linked to the Ashton B. Samlesbury-bodied Leyland PD1A No. 98 is seen on the Jacson Street stand, *c.* 1959/60. (MRC)

The BF/FR/LS all took the number 36 in the 1980 renumbering scheme. In June 1983 the Fulwood Row journeys were withdrawn and were replaced by service 37, which was routed via Garstang Road. The 36 continued to run via Deepdale Road as displayed on the blind of Leyland Panther No. 224, seen in Watling Street Road on 10 January 1981.

The CR was given the number 35 as depicted by Alexander-bodied Leyland Atlantean No. 110, which is seen in Cromwell Road crossing the long-closed Preston to Longridge railway on 19 December 1981. The service was subjected to a three-year diversion via Deepdale Road due to a weight restriction being placed on this bridge; this was lifted in September 1973.

Service 6 (renumbered from 36) was withdrawn on 13 July 1987 but then reinstated on 12 October with operation by minibuses. At the same time, it was rerouted around the Brookfield estate. It continued to operate, with minor alterations, until 21 October 2006. Service 7 (renumbered from 37) was then altered to cover the section of route around the estate. The district was also served by the Orbit routes 88A/C. Northern Counties-bodied Dodge S56 No. 72 is seen crossing the railway overbridge in Deepdale Road, with MCW Metrorider No. 24 in pursuit, on 7 March 1996.

Showing Gamull Lane, by the time this picture was recorded of English Electric-bodied Leyland Lion No. 83 it would actually have been bound for Fulwood Row, as the terminus became known from 1 January 1948. The town centre stand was moved from Lancaster Road to Harris Street, where No. 83 is waiting time circa 1950, and then again moved to Jacson Street in May 1954, one month after the last two Lions were withdrawn from service. (MRC)

The Fulwood Row journeys were replaced by a new route 37, which ran via Garstang Road from 13 June 1983. This then became the 7 and was converted to minibus operation from 13 July 1987. Between May 2001 and October 2006 the estate section of the route was omitted, with buses running direct along Watling Street Road. Former Lothian Buses Leyland Olympian No. 129 was photographed at the Fulwood Row terminus on 24 August 2005.

Following the acquisition of Preston Bus by Stagecoach in January 2009 service 7 was retained but reverted back to Preston Bus in March 2010. However, from 7 June the 7 was withdrawn, with the Brookfield area subsequently served by an extension of service 14 from Ronaldsway to Croasdale Avenue while new Stagecoach service 4A covered the section of route from the city centre to Sharoe Green Lane. Repainted Preston Optare Solo No. 47787 is seen in Lancaster Road on 18 February 2009.

The 14 was further extended from Croasdale Avenue to Fulwood Row from 3 September 2012. However, from 4 April 2016 the service was altered to serve Longsands vice Brookfield, with the latter henceforth served by a new service 6/6A running via Deepdale Road. The last Lynx in service is about to turn from Cromwell Road into Ronaldsway with an additional early morning departure from Brookfield on 16 July 2013.

The final chapter in the somewhat convoluted story of services to Brookfield dates from 4 April 2016 when services 6/6A commenced running via the original BF route but extended beyond Fulwood Row to the Red Scar industrial estate. The 6A was the evening and Sunday variant, which turned back at Gamull Lane. Initially operated by minibuses, larger buses were later introduced. Rotala Preston Bus (carrying a Diamond fleetname) ELC-bodied Scania Omnidekka No. 40415 is seen in Deepdale Road on 3 April 2019.

Cottam

Until the mid-1980s Cottam was still an expanse of open farmland. The construction of Tom Benson Way and Cottam Way opened up new transport links, and over the last twenty-five years the district has seen vast areas of residential development. Predating the housebuilding explosion, Northern Counties-bodied Renault S56 No. 86 is pictured in Cottam Way on 15 July 1996. A handful of peak-time journeys on services 34 and 43 were extended from/to Cottam from that date running under the service numbers 134 and 143. These remained in the timetable until May 2001 and June 2004 respectively.

The route number 36 was recycled for a second time from 27 October 1997 when every third departure on minibus service 32 to Tanterton was renumbered and extended to Cottam Way/ Valentines Meadow. As the road network developed the service was rerouted from 12 February 2001 to loop via Merry Trees Lane and Haydock Lane. Just over a year later the terminal point was moved to the Ancient Oak PH. Following the introduction of the Orbit routes in October 2006 the service was cut back to Tanterton. The 36 was withdrawn after 28 July 2007, apart from a single school journey that operated using the number 136. Former Lothian Buses Olympian No. 125 is seen at Withy Trees on 11 July 2005 working the aforementioned journey, which was finally withdrawn in 2010.

From 4 April 2016 the service number 43 was reintroduced for a new service to Cottam that ran via Mill Lane (replacing service 80, which had commenced on 14 April 2014) and the Ingol estate and terminated in Cottam Way. This was a partial replacement for the Cottam section of the Orbit routes, which were withdrawn at the same time. This service was short-lived and replaced by the reintroduction of service 44, which was extended via Cottam Way and Sidgreaves Lane to Hoyles Lane at Cottam. Optare Solo No. 20789 is seen in Lancaster Road on the first day of operation, 5 September 2016.

The number 26 had only previously been used once before for services to Lea in the 1980s. The short-lived service, which operated via Lea Road and Cottam to Nog Tow between 26 September and 7 December 2017, was the first bus service to operate under Waterloo Railway Bridge (height restricted until April 1984) since March 1954. Slimline Optare Solo No. 20811 is seen climbing away from the bridge in Waterloo Road on the first day of operation; St Walburge's Church steeple is again prominent in the distance.

As development in the Cottam area continued to expand, the 44 service was joined by a new service, which again used the number 43. Commencing operation on 19 July 2020 it was routed via the railway station, Pedder Street and Tom Benson Way before continuing via Hoyles Lane and Lightfoot Lane to the RPH. Optare Solo SR No. 20702, repainted in the new Rotala Preston Bus livery, was photographed in Sidgreaves Lane at Lea on 26 September 2020 on an inbound journey. The road layout at this location has since been significantly altered.

Farringdon Park

Farringdon Park Pleasure Gardens was initially served by a horse-drawn tramway, which commenced operation on 14 April 1882. A newly constructed electric tramway replaced the latter from 7 June 1904. This was abandoned on 4 July 1932 when a new batch of ten English Electric-bodied Leyland TD2s was introduced to the FP and P services. Crossley-bodied Leyland PD2/10 No. 31 is seen at the Tudor Avenue (originally known as Thornville Road) terminus, at the junction of New Hall Lane, on 30 September 1976. This has been the terminus for the route since January 1964, although both the horse-drawn and electric trams used to terminate on the main road, virtually in front of the bus.

New in 1959, MCCW-bodied Leyland PD3/5 No. 68 is seen passing the cemetery gates at the junction of New Hall Lane and Blackpool Road on 7 August 1976. From here it is only a short distance to the terminus. Through running from/to Queens Drive continued until 7 August 1978 when the PL was converted to OPO. The terminus for the Cemetery to Lane Ends services was in Blackpool Road, approximately where the lighting column is located.

The FP service assumed the service number 16 from 3 November 1980. Following deregulation, alternate journeys on Saturdays only were extended to the railway station using the service number 116. These interworked with similar extended journeys from Ribbleton, which ran as service 111. This arrangement lasted from 1 November 1986 until 11 July 1987. ELC-bodied Atlantean No. 133 was photographed alongside the Butler Street entrance to the station on 13 June 1987.

When the FP was first converted to motorbus operation the buses turned by reversing into Tudor Avenue (unthinkable today). Between February 1949 and May 1963, the terminus stand was on the opposite side of New Hall Lane, in Farringdon Crescent. It was then altered back to Tudor Avenue, with the buses returning via Cairnsmore Avenue. The direction of travel at the terminus was reversed in January 1964 and has remained the same ever since. Former Lothian Buses Leyland Olympian No. 128 is seen in Cairnsmore Avenue on 5 June 2006.

The 16 was the last route to employ conductors and was converted to OPO on 22 March 1982. Having been predominantly worked by double-deckers, low-floor Scanias with East Lancashire Esteem bodies were introduced from 4 July 2007. One of the type, No. 28510 (Preston Bus No. 200), is seen during the brief Stagecoach period of operation in Cairnsmore Avenue on 18 March 2009. This bus could still be found working on this route in early 2021, although by then under Rotala ownership.

The original FP bus stand was outside Miller Arcade in Church Street. It was moved to outside the Town Hall (later the site of Crystal House) in October 1954 and then to Bay 16 at the bus station fifteen years later. The route was linked with the Broadgate (Penwortham) until August 1953 after which it was linked with the PL. The FP/16 had remained largely unaltered until July 2021 when it was linked with the Larches (89) and the joint service was renumbered to 100. The route however remained unaltered. One of Rotala's former FirstBus Volvo B7RLEs, No. 69180, is seen in New Hall Lane on 26 July 2021, 139 years after the service first started running.

Callon

To the south of New Hall Lane (served by the FP/16) lie the districts of Fishwick and Callon, with neither having had their own bus service for any length of time. The Callon estate was built between the two world wars and was briefly served by the CL service from 30 August 1976 until 1 July 1977 on Monday to Friday only. Having worked through from Savick, Duple-bodied Bristol LHS No. 242 is seen in Earl Street on 31 August 1976 and after calling in at the bus station it would have worked the next duty to Callon.

Fulwood

The Plungington service (later PL) was the first bus service to be introduced, on 23 January 1922. The original stand was alongside the Town Hall in Birley Street and the inaugural service was operated by English Electric-bodied, thirty-seat Leyland G7s. Double-deck types were first introduced to the route in August 1926. Leyland TD1 No. 66 was photographed in the Market Square when new in late 1928. (MRC)

For a brief period, until 30 November 1922, the service ran as a circular running out via Brook Street and returning via Plungington Road. It was then altered to run out and back via Plungington Road to the junction of Lytham Road (which was actually just in the urban district of Fulwood) where it turned in the wide expanse of the junction. An unidentified pre-war Leyland Titan can be seen at the terminus in Black Bull Lane in this 1934 view. Alternate buses had been extended to Boys Lane from 3 July 1933. (MRC)

English Electric-bodied Leyland TD4c No. 16 is seen on the PL stand in Birley Street sometime during the early 1950s. The PL stand was moved several times, having been in Birley Street, Church Street and Harris Street before being relocated, as seen above, in January 1948. From 17 August 1953 it was moved back to Church Street, latterly outside the parish church, where it remained until its relocation to the bus station in 1969. (MRC)

Lytham Road had been abandoned as a terminus in August 1936 and a further extension to the route, to Queens Drive, was made in March 1939, with alternate buses continuing to turn back at Boys Lane. In this view of Leyland PD2/10 No. 43, in experimental livery of Oxford blue and white, the bus is showing Farringdon Park as the PL was at the time linked with the FP. No. 43 is pictured in an almost deserted Black Bull Lane in 1967. (MRC)

From May 1973 the Boys Lane terminus was abandoned with all buses running through to Queens Drive. At its height the PL had operated to a five-minute frequency and since each terminus required a reversing manoeuvre it made operational sense to use two different terminal points. MCCW-bodied Leyland PD3/5 No. 64 is passing the temporary Guild stands in the Market Square in the first week of September 1972. (MRC)

MCCW-bodied Leyland PD3A/1 No. 86 had just reversed off Black Bull Lane into Queens Drive when it was photographed on 4 December 1977. At the time reversing manoeuvres were still required at Fulwood Row (FR), Holme Slack (HS), Hutton (P5), Longsands Lane (LS) and Savick Luton Road (P7) as well as at Queens Drive. This location ceased to be used as a terminus after 6 August 1978 when the route was further extended to RPH.

At the same time as the extension was made to a new turning circle in Sharoe Green Lane, adjacent to the then newly built Royal Preston Hospital (RPH), the PL was also converted to OPO using dual-door Atlanteans. This was the second double-deck conversion following the GL service in August 1976. For a brief period the turning circle was also used by the extended 15 and 20 services before they were further extended to Sherwood/Asda. On 18 June 1983 ELC-bodied Leyland Atlantean No. 152 was keeping company with similar vehicle No. 133, which was on the 15, at the RPH terminus.

From 13 July 1987 the 22 was replaced in the evening and on Sunday by new services 123/23, which ran through to Sherwood/Fulwood Asda. Low-floor buses were introduced to the interworked routes from the end of May 2001. The service number 22 was dropped from 30 July 2007 but then reintroduced from 19 May 2008. Dennis Trident No. 18588, repainted in Preston Citi Stagecoach livery, is seen departing the bus station on 26 March 2009. This Trident continued in service with Rotala Preston Bus until January 2019.

Under Stagecoach ownership the 22 was briefly linked with the 19, forming a circular service. From 7 June 2010 it was reduced to just a number of one-way, peak-time journeys, the last of which were finally removed from the timetable after 2 April 2016, with all journeys henceforth running with the service number 23. In 2013 Rotala took eight Volvo hybrid buses on a seven-year lease and these were generally employed on the 23. No. 40607, which was dedicated to the memory of *Sir Tom Finney*, was reposing at the RPH terminus on 22 March 2016. The turning circle was still in use in 2021 – by the 88.

As previously mentioned, a further extension to the Plungington route was implemented from 13 July 1987, with alternate buses being extended to the newly opened Asda store at Fulwood using the service number 23. These ran as 123 when buses only went as far as Sherwood. Throughout over 100 years of operation the Plungington service has been predominantly worked by double-deckers and to a high frequency. The Sunday 123 service did see a more frequent use of single-deck buses as represented by Leyland Lynx No. 18, which was photographed at the Sherwood terminus on 22 July 1990. From 29 May 2001 Sherwood ceased to be used as a terminus and the service number 123 was dropped.

From October 1997 the last two late-night departures were extended beyond Asda to Longsands Lane (service number 23 reused). On the night of Friday 22 January 2009, Lynx No. 212 and Olympian No. 133 performed the last rites for Preston Bus before the takeover by Stagecoach the following day. Following the ruling by the Competition Commission, Stagecoach had to relinquish their ownership of Preston Bus and the operator was sold on to Rotala in January 2011. No. 133 is pictured in the rain at Asda on the last day; Lynx No. 212 is out of sight behind.

Service 23 continued to run under Rotala ownership with just one minor alteration to the route. In January 1990 the route had been altered to run via Oliver's Place and Pittman Way in both directions, vice Eastway. From 4 April 2016 inbound buses from Asda were altered to run via Eastway to Sherwood Way. The Volvo hybrid buses had dominated the service for seven years but from mid-2020 four micro-hybrid Wrightbus Streetdecks were introduced to the route. A further four of the type, with route branding, were added the following year. No. 40805 is seen in Plungington Road on 18 May 2021; the diminutive G7s would have passed the same houses ninety-nine years previously.

An electric tram service commenced running on 30 June 1904 from Lancaster Road, routed via Church Street and Deepdale Road to Watling Street Road. The following month it was extended to run as a circular route returning to town via Garstang Road and North Road. Later operating as service D, buses replaced the trams from 16 December 1935. Samlesbury-bodied Leyland PD1A No. 100 is seen outside the Transport Offices in Lancaster Road, sometime in the mid-1950s. (MRC)

The D and the F circulars were converted to OPO on 2 December 1968. They were also the first services to trial the exact-fare method of payment, in October 1973, following the initial trial fitment of coin-in-the slot fareboxes to six Leyland Panthers. This method of fare collection was soon rolled out to all OPO routes and remained in use until July 2021. Seddon-bodied Panther No. 235 is seen at the Watling Street Road stand on 31 January 1981, by which date the route had been renumbered to 15.

After nearly eighty years of running as a circular service, from 13 June 1983 the D/15 was altered to run via Sharoe Green Lane to the RPH turning circle and return using the outbound route. From 2 January 1985 it was further extended via the newly constructed Sherwood Way to turn at the junction of Eastway. In August 1986 certain journeys were extended to Fulwood Asda running as the 115. The route was withdrawn in its entirety following the service changes of 12 July 1987. ELC-bodied Atlantean No. 177 was caught on camera in Sherwood Way on 22 April 1985.

A horse-drawn tram route to Fulwood (Barracks) commenced running via North Road, Garstang Road and Victoria Road on 20 March 1879. It was worked by local business concern Hardings on behalf of the Preston Tramways Company. This ceased to operate after 31 December 1903 and was replaced by an electric tram service, which commenced operation on 7 June 1904 and operated via Watling Street Road to Victoria Road. In conjunction with the anticlockwise service, it was altered to run as a circular from the following month. Assuming the route letter F, *c.* 1930, Leyland PD3A/1 No. 70 is seen westbound in Church Street in this late 1960s view, before the road was made one-way in the opposite direction. (MRC)

The history of the clockwise route follows that of the anticlockwise route from June 1983 onwards. From November 1980 it ran as service 20. The two services were also the first routes on which Atlanteans – from the Nos 101–10 batch – ran as OPO buses. ELC-bodied Atlantean No. 128 is seen turning from Watling Street Road (since renamed Sir Tom Finney Way) into Deepdale Road on 2 August 1981, with Fulwood Barracks as a backdrop.

Now numbered 20, the former circular route is seen being worked by ELC-bodied Atlantean No. 170, which was photographed turning from Sharoe Green Lane into Watling Street Road on 13 June 1983 on its return journey from Sherwood. Extended journeys to Fulwood Asda ran as service 120.

After deregulation the minibus revolution took hold from April 1987. An entirely new route, numbered 19, commenced running on 21 April using Northern Counties-bodied twenty-two-seat Dodge S56 minibuses. From 1 June the service ran every five minutes and operated out via the previous service 15 routing to RPH, but also included a section of running around Levensgarth Avenue, Longfield and Broadwood Drive before terminating in the hospital grounds. Dodge S46 No. 69 is seen in Lancaster Road on 17 July 1987.

From April 1988 the section of route along Levensgarth Avenue and Longfield was omitted, and buses ran the full length of Broadwood Drive. ELC-bodied Dodge S56 No. 8 had previously operated for Barrow Borough Transport and Stagecoach before being acquired to operate the Port Way Park & Ride service. It is seen in Broadwood Drive on 8 August 1994, having by then been repainted into fleet colours.

In December 2001 eight Optare Solos joined the fleet, which were adorned with route branding for the 19. They took over from the smaller minibuses on 2 January 2002. No. 54 is seen in Sir Tom Finney Way (previously Deepdale Road) on the third day of operation. At the time six buses were required to maintain the service.

Following the takeover by Stagecoach, from 22 March 2009 the 19 was linked with the 22, swapping over outside Booths in Sharoe Green Lane. Service 19A was introduced at the same time and replaced the 19 round the Sharoe Green estate but there was no evening or Sunday service. It regained the number 19 from 7 June 2010 (when through running with the 22 was discontinued), but the number 19A remained in use for the Sunday and evening service, which omitted the estate. From May 2012 the 19 and 19A ran throughout the day as alternate departures, but this was short-lived as all journeys became 19A from 4 March 2013 and finally renumbered back to 19 from 4 April 2016. Rotala Preston Bus Optare Versa No. 30131 was photographed in Sharoe Green Lane on 14 January 2016.

Representing the present-day service is former Hallmark Scania OmniCity No. 40515, which is seen on the 19 stand in the hospital grounds on 20 July 2020. A seventy-eight-seat double-decker is somewhat of a step up from a twenty-two-seat minibus. The estate ceased to be served from 4 April 2016, having been substantially reduced in March 2013.

A short-lived service to Conway Drive in Fulwood was the 24. It ran from 17 August to 9 October 1987 with operation by dedicated Dodge S56 No. 44. This bus was received with two fewer seats than the others of the type and was equipped with extra baggage space. No. 44 was photographed in Black Bull Lane on 31 August 1987.

Conway Drive was again the ultimate destination for another minibus service, which ran as the 28 between 19 October 1998 and 12 June 2004. The route was fairly similar to the erstwhile 24, via North Road and Garstang Road until it turned off at Black Bull Lane, while the 24 had gone a little further north before turning into Brookside Road. Park & Ride-branded Optare Solo No. 65 was somewhat unusually employed on the service on 12 June 2004 (the last day of operation) and is seen in Conway Drive.

Following the withdrawal of the 28, new service 45 commenced running from Janice Drive from 14 June 2004. The service consisted of just one inbound journey on Monday to Friday. It was routed via Black Bull Lane and Sharoe Green Lane to Watling Street Road. From 19 May 2008 it was substantially rerouted via Black Bull Lane, Plungington Road and Adelphi Street. Normally the preserve of big buses, ELC-bodied Leyland Atlantean No. 174 is seen in Conway Drive on 11 July 2005. The service ran for the last time on 30 August 2008.

In compensation for the loss of the 19 from the Sharoe Green estate (other than a handful of early morning journeys) a new service numbered 4B, supported by Lancashire County Council and operated by Preston Bus, commenced operation on 4 March 2013. This was short-lived and was replaced by rerouting Stagecoach service 4A from 1 July 2013. Wrightbus Streetlite No. 20908 was in charge of the service on 29 May 2013.

Another short-lived service was the 5, which ran to the North Eastern Employment Area in Fulwood. Commencing on 30 January 2017, there were initially just three evening peak-time inbound journeys. From 27 March a limited outbound service was provided in the early morning, which was reduced to a single journey from 28 January 2019. Former Lothian Buses Dennis Trident No. 40541 is seen in Watling Street Road on 20 March 2017 with a tea-time working to the bus station. The service was suspended from 27 March 2020 due to the Covid-19 pandemic, and remained so at the time of writing.

The Orbit services ran seven days a week until 9 September 2012 when they were withdrawn on a Sunday. While the route was partly covered by service 89 to Larches in the west, new service 86 was introduced to cover the eastern section of the route as far as RPH. Optare Solo No. 20787 was photographed passing the Preston North End fixture board in Sir Tom Finney Way on 15 February 2015. The service ran for the last time on 3 April 2016. Manchester United won the fifth round FA Cup tie by three goals to one.

A number of service changes took place on 20 July 2020, which saw two new services serve the Royal Preston Hospital. *Above*: The number 43 was reintroduced for a service that was routed via the railway station, Pedder Street, Tom Benson Way, Wychnor, Lightfoot Lane and Garstang Road to RPH. On Sundays it only ran as far as Wychnor. Optare Solo No. 20782 is seen on Fishergate Bridge on 28 July 2020. *Below*: Service 49 replaced the section of service 15 that ran via Deepdale Road and Watling Street Road to Longsands and Fulwood Asda; from there the 49 then continued via Pittman Way, Easway, Longfield and Broadwood Drive to RPH. Former Maltese Government Optare Solo SR No. 20879 was recorded in the hospital grounds on the first day of operation. The 49 was linked with the 88 for operational purposes. Behind is Scania Omnidekka No. 40411 on service 19.

From 1 January 1948 a number of jointly operated services (with Ribble & Scout) commenced running to localities just outside the borough boundary. One such route was the P2, which ran from the Plough Inn at Penwortham to Lightfoot Lane in Fulwood. It was successively extended along Lightfoot Lane to Hazelmere Road (in 1964), Lansdown Hill (in 1970 when it was also converted to OPO) and finally to a new turning circle in Lightfoot Lane in May 1977. Ribble had always provided the buses from the end of 1948 until 17 April 1978 when the route was swapped for the P5 (renumbered to P50 at the time), at which time it reverted back to a full crewed service. *Above*: Ribble Alexander-bodied Leyland PDR1/2 No. 1867 (with conductor) was photographed in Lightfoot Lane on 29 November 1977. *Below*: Borough of Preston Leyland PD3 Rebuild No. 59 is seen in a deserted Garstang Road (A6) on the same service on Monday 17 April 1978.

Through running to Penwortham ceased with the change of operator. The turning circle became the official terminus from 12 November 1977. From 7 August 1978 the service was converted to OPO in the evening, while full OPO was implemented from 3 November 1980, at which time the route assumed the service number 28. ELC-bodied Atlantean No. 119 was caught on camera at the Lightfoot Lane terminus on 23 February 1983. The route was extended through to Tanterton from 13 June 1983.

Frenchwood

The Frenchwood service was the Corporation's second bus route and commenced running on 5 June 1924. It was inaugurated in lieu of further tramway expansion and ran as a circular service until 6 December 1928 when it was extended to Ashworth Grove at Lower Frenchwood. It assumed the service letters FR *c*. 1930 and was linked with the Ashton D from 8 April 1947. The original stand was in Birley Street, but it was moved to Jacson Street in January 1948 where it remained until January 1961. Leyland PD2/10 No. 47 is seen on the town centre stand in the late 1950s. (MRC)

From 1 January 1948 the FR/D became the jointly operated P1, which ran from Carlton Drive at Frenchwood via the town centre, railway station and Ashton Lane Ends to Victoria Park Drive at Lea. The original P1 stand was in Jacson Street until January 1961 when it was moved to Lancaster Road. The Birley Street stand, where Crossley-bodied Leyland PD2/10 No. 25 is depicted, was used by the P1/P3 from February 1964 until the new bus station opened. Journeys from/to Lea were renumbered to P3 from 15 February 1965. (MRC)

Ribble provided one bus in the timetable schedule from the start of the agreement until the service was converted to OPO on 6 April 1970; thereafter the Corporation provided the full complement of buses. The only significant alteration to the route was the reversal of the direction of travel on Manchester Road and Grimshaw Street in December 1973. Marshall-bodied Leyland Panther No. 212 was photographed in Lancaster Road on 27 September 1980.

Joint operation of the Frenchwood service ceased on 3 November 1980 and the route was split from the Larches/Lea running under the service number 29. From 11 April 1988 the service was partially converted to operation using minibuses. However, Preston Bus ceased to operate the service after 15 October 1989. ELC-bodied coach-seated Atlantean No. 2 is seen turning from London Road into Ashworth Grove on 30 July 1983.

Thereafter the district was served by a number of independent bus operators, including Fylde Borough Transport, until the service was reintroduced by Stagecoach on 22 June 2009. This in turn was continued by Preston Bus from March 2010, but was withdrawn by Rotala after 21 July 2012 when services 112 (Leyland) and 114 (Chorley) were diverted to run via Frenchwood. Between 11 December 2017 and 16 February 2019, the 29 was reintroduced, thus replacing the 112 (the 114 had ceased to run after 2 April 2016) over this period. Optare Solo No. 20780 is seen in Ashworth Grove on 18 December 2017.

When the Frenchwood service first commenced, buses ran every twenty minutes. By the 1950s the frequency of the service had increased to every ten minutes. From 11 December 2017 only a basic hourly service was provided by the diversion of service 112, which ran to Bamber Bridge via Leyland. The various services had been financed by Lancashire County Council for a number of years and the contract to operate the 112 was awarded to Holmeswood Coaches from 18 July 2020. Optare Solo No. 20776 is seen in Ashworth Grove on 29 November 2017.

Ribbleton Gamull Lane

Electric trams had provided a service to Ribbleton from 26 January 1905. The trams were phased out between September 1932 and June 1934, with buses progressively taking over. One of the first tramway replacement buses, English Electric-bodied Leyland TD2 No. 49, can be seen on the Ribbleton stand alongside the impressive Miller Shopping Arcade in this picture, which dates from the mid-1930s. In later years the bobby used to stand in a raised box to direct the traffic. No. 49 was loaned to the London Passenger Transport Board in 1940/1. (MRC)

Pristine-looking Leyland-bodied PD1A No. 91 is seen on the Ribbleton stand in Church Street in this early 1950s view. By this time the use of the service letter R had all but been discontinued, other than for a few short journeys, as the bulk of the service used the letters GL/P5 from January 1948. The trams had departed from more or less the same spot, from September 1932, and this remained the stand for the GL until December 1960 after which the GL/P5 departed from a stand in Jacson Street. (MRC)

For many years the GL/P5 service turned round at the junction of Longridge Road and Gamull Lane by means of performing a circle in the wide expanse of the junction. MCCW-bodied Leyland PD2/10 No. 83 was photographed making the manoeuvre on 13 July 1976. A restricted-width bridge was situated just beyond the houses on the right and crossed the long-closed railway line to Longridge. It was later demolished in the 1980s, thereby opening up new opportunities for bus routes including the 6/A, 14 and 88A/C.

The jointly operated P5 service was inaugurated on 1 January 1948. Buses ran through from the Anchor Inn at Hutton to Ribbleton Gamull Lane. Every third bus from town to Ribbleton ran as a P5 as opposed to a GL. Apart from in the first year of operation the buses were always provided by Preston. MCCW-bodied Leyland PD3A/1 No. 88 is seen at the top of Penwortham Hill, working back from Hutton on the last day of operation, 15 April 1978. The following day the route was renumbered P50 and taken over by Ribble.

The GL route was converted to OPO on 30 August 1976, at which time the P5 to Hutton (which remained crew-operated) became a separate route for operational purposes, starting from the bus station, although the GL was still technically jointly operated. Usually worked by Atlanteans, the appearance of a Leyland Panther was not uncommon. Seddon-bodied Panther No. 225 is seen at the Gamull Lane terminus in Longridge Road on 20 May 1977. Ribble Albion Lowlander No. 1860 is seen behind on service 8 from Longridge.

From 3 November 1980 the GL became service 10. It continued to turn round at the junction of Gamull Lane and Longridge Road until it was replaced by service 11. ELC-bodied Atlantean No. 138 has just set down its passengers before turning round on 12 April 1982. Between October 1989 and January 1990, a handful of early morning journeys worked to and from the Roman Way industrial estate.

The service number 11 was introduced when some journeys were rerouted at Ribbleton to turn in a one-way loop via part of the Grange estate from 13 June 1983. The service number 10 was dropped when all journeys were thus routed from 13 July 1987. Freshly repainted former demonstrator ECW-bodied Leyland Olympian No. 133 was photographed in Lords Walk arriving back from Ribbleton on 13 October 1999.

East Lancashire Coachbuilder's Omnidekka, which was mounted on a Scania chassis, was in production between 2003 and 2011. Demonstrator YN54 OCY spent two weeks working on the usual test-bed route, the 11, as seen on 24 August 2005. Preston Bus later purchased two former Omnidekka demonstrators with another five joining the Rotala Preston Bus fleet in 2019.

New low-floor Scania Esteems were introduced to the route on 4 September 2006. Early morning/evening and Sunday journeys were altered to continue to Bluebell Way roundabout to turn. This practice continued until 12 November 2007 from when all journeys were again routed via the Grange estate. No. 205 is seen in Grange Avenue on the second day of operation, 5 September.

Grange

When first introduced, the Grange estate route was an entirely new concept. Three Duple-bodied Bristol LHS minibuses, Nos 242–4, were specially purchased in May 1976 to operate two new routes and convert a third route to OPO. All three routes commenced operation on 30 August. In the interim the buses were used as extras on a variety of routes, usually operating with a conductor. Non-appearance of the type was quite rare, but Seddon-bodied Panther No. 235, seen in Lancaster Road, was deputising for a Bristol on 25 April 1980.

Showing the wrong service number (should be 12) the normal type of bus for the service, Bristol LHS No. 344 (formerly No. 244), is seen in the same location on New Year's Day 1981. Following the withdrawal of the Callon service only two Bristols were required and services 12 and 30 were linked for operational purposes. The route was withdrawn with the introduction of bus deregulation on 24 October 1986.

A new route around the Grange estate, taking the relinquished number 10, commenced running on 10 December 1992. It first did a double run through the bus station to serve Ormskirk Road and then took the direct route along Ribbleton Lane/ Avenue. It then travelled round the estate in the opposite direction to the previous estate route. MCW Metrorider No. 6 is seen in Grange Avenue on 18 May 1998, with Lynx No. 210 behind on service 11. The service was withdrawn after 11 June 2004.

Holme Slack

The Holme Slack HS service commenced running on 17 February 1936. It was linked with the Lane Ends Ashton C between October 1943 and December 1972. The original bus stand was in Lancaster Road, but it was moved several times, including to Jacson Street and Birley Street (three times). For many years normal fare on the HS/C were the Corporation's PD1/As. Alexander-bodied No. 52 is seen in Lancaster Road, *c*, 1959. Leyland PD2/1 No. 116, behind, was withdrawn in April 1970 and was used by the Earby Pothole Club as transport for an expedition to Simla, in the Himalaya foothills. (MRC/John Conway)

There was very little alteration to the route of the HS (other than relocation to the bus station) until April 1978 when a new turning circle was commissioned to eliminate the reversing manoeuvre into Lily Grove. There then followed a brief period of through running to Farringdon Park, between August 1978 and January 1980. MCCW-bodied Leyland PD3A/1 No. 71 was photographed at the new terminus on 19 August 1978.

The HS was converted to OPO on 14 January 1980 and was then allotted the service number 14 in November. No further changes took place until 13 July 1987 when the 14 was withdrawn in the evening and on Sunday, at which time it was replaced by new minibus-operated service 114. ELC-bodied Leyland Atlantean No. 123 has just left the Holme Slack Lane terminus on 20 February 1982. Lily Grove can be seen on the left behind the bus.

Service 114 was introduced on 11 May 1987 and followed the route of the 14 to the end of Holme Slack Lane but then continued along Ronaldsway to Fairfax Road at Ribbleton. Ronaldsway was only connected to Holme Slack Lane in the 1970s and was really considered to be too narrow for a bus service. Nevertheless, it supported a variety of minibus services until 2018. Northern Counties-bodied Dodge S56 No. 60 had just left the terminus when photographed on 25 May 1987. Brookfield estate is in the distance.

From 13 July 1987 the 114 was altered to serve Romford Road. From 27 October 1997 the 14 was also converted to minibus operation and extended to Fairfax Road (the turning circle was abandoned except for school bus journeys). The two routes then continued to run in tandem until 29 May 2001 when the 114 was withdrawn. The service was acquired by Stagecoach on 23 January 2009 but reverted back to Preston Bus on 15 March 2010 with no service being provided in the evening or on Sunday. It was later reinstated at these times from 7 June 2010 with financial support from the county council and operated by Stagecoach. Optare Solo No. 47656 is seen in Lambert Road on Sunday 5 May 2013.

Following the period of full operation by Stagecoach the service was first extended to Brookfield, on 7 June 2010, and then to Fulwood Row, on 3 September 2012, although in the evening and on Sunday it continued to terminate at Fairfax Road. For a period in 2013 it ran beyond Fulwood Row to turn round at the Gamull Lane/Longridge Road junction. Heading for Fulwood Row, but still using the Brookfield destination, Optare Solo No. 20787 was caught on camera in Sedgwick Street on 22 April 2015.

Further rerouting took place from 4 April 2016 when the service was altered to serve Longsands, vice Brookfield (Fulwood Row). This arrangement lasted until 1 September 2018 when the 14 was cut back to terminate at Holme Slack Lane, as it had done between 1936 and 1997. Optare Solo No. 20792 is seen in Watling Street Road on 20 March 2017 on the 14A, which was a peak-time variant of the 14.

Ingol

The jointly operated P4 service to Ingol commenced running on 13 February 1965. It was somewhat unusual in that the service departed from the Express Coach Station at the corner of Lords Walk and North Road. This arrangement lasted until the station was closed to make way for the construction of the new bus station. MCCW-bodied Leyland PD3A/1 No. 85 has just pulled off the stand in this view, which dates from around 1966/7. (Ribble Enthusiasts Club/ Peter Whitworth)

When the service was first introduced buses turned round at the junction of Cottam Avenue and Barry Avenue. From 25 June 1966 a number of journeys were extended around the estate, but the full timetable didn't follow suit until 7 November 1970. Prior to 1973 the Sunday service had only run in the afternoon and additionally was exclusively provide by Ribble until May 1980. Crossley-bodied Leyland PD2/10 No. 31 is seen waiting to turn from Cottam Avenue into Tag Lane with the 08.13 to town on 16 July 1976.

During the week the Ribble duties were confined to certain peak-time departures. On 8 November 1976 Ribble MCCW-bodied Leyland PDR1/1 Atlantean No. 1686 is seen departing the bus station at 17.35. The shoe was now on the other foot as the joint Ingol services (P4 and P6) were the only Ribble-operated routes, which used the west side of the bus station.

The P4 was converted to OPO from 1 October 1976, although certain peak-time journeys remained crew-operated until 3 November 1980, at which time the route was also numbered 34. However, the evening and Sunday service was provided by the 44, which was routed via Brook Street and Blackpool Road. Modified Alexander-bodied Leyland Atlantean No. 106 was photographed at Ashton Lane Ends on 7 May 1984.

From 13 July 1987 the route was altered to run via Redcar Avenue and Whitby Avenue from Cottam Avenue, at Ingol, and from 16 October 1989 minibuses took over operation of the route. Only minor alterations to the route in the town centre followed until the service was withdrawn after 28 July 2007; it was replaced by the 44 but with no evening or Sunday service. Northern Counties-bodied Renault S56 No. 48 was caught on camera in Redcar Avenue on 9 August 1995.

Service 44 to Ingol initially only ran in the evening and on Sunday in conjunction with the 33 to Tanterton. From 16 July 1989 it ran as a daily service with minibus operation; however, it reverted back to operation with standard-size buses in the evening and on Sunday from 27 October 1997. Various minor alterations to the route had taken place, including inbound working via Plungington Road and Adelphi Street between July 1987 and June 2004 and again from 30 July 2007, before the route was taken over by Stagecoach on 23 January 2009. ELC-bodied Leyland Atlantean No. 177 is seen in Woodplumpton Road at Lane Ends on Sunday 21 May 1989.

From 19 May 2008 the outbound journeys were also routed through Plungington. Stagecoach repainted a number of former Preston Bus Solos with 'Citi' branding before they were instructed to cease repainting buses. Former Preston Bus No. 477(61), originally obtained in December 2002 for the Park & Ride services and the one thousandth Solo built by Optare (plaque mounted behind the driver's cab) is seen departing the bus station for Ingol in March 2009.

The service was transferred back to Preston Bus on 15 March 2010. From 18 November 2013 the 44 returned to two-way operation along Brook Street. However, it was withdrawn after 2 April 2016, with Ingol then being served by a reincarnation of service 43, which ran via Mill Lane and the Ingol estate before continuing to Cottam. In this busy scene, recorded in Tag Lane at Ingol on 10 July 2015, Scania Esteem No. 30920 is causing somewhat of a holdup as it picks up passengers on the Tanterton service. However, the driver of Optare Solo No. 20786 has decided not to wait and is heading back to the bus station from Ingol. Another Solo and a Scania Omnidekka wait patiently behind.

This version of the 43 was short-lived and the 44 was reintroduced from 5 September 2016. Again, routed via Brook Street, the route served the Ingol estate and then continued to Cottam, where it turned round at Lea Road roundabout. From 3 September 2018 it was extended to prescribe a clockwise loop along Sidgreaves Lane and Hoyles Lane back to Tag Lane. On 25 January 2019 Rotala Preston Bus Wright-bodied Volvo B9TL No. 40503 (formerly with Rotala Wessex) was making an unusual appearance on the normally minibus-worked 44 and is seen in Redcar Avenue.

The convoluted story of the Ingol service took another twist on 20 July 2020. From this date the route was altered in the city centre to run along Fishergate and Corporation Street and further altered at its extremity to loop through Cottam in the opposite direction. Optare Solo SR No. 20702 was about to turn from Fishergate into Corporation Street when photographed on 26 July 2020. Following the lengthy planned closure of Corporation Street for road improvement works the 44 was further altered to run via Friargate from 18 October 2020 with further route alterations taking place from 15 March 2021, along with services 23 and 31, following the reopening of Adelphi Street and the temporary closure of Brook Street.

A second jointly operated, somewhat limited, service commenced running to the Ingol estate on 12 November 1973. The original route served Walker Street, Fylde Road, Tulketh Brow and Woodplumpton Road. However, from 24 November 1975, the route was radically altered to run via North Road, Garstang Road, Lytham Road, Black Bull Lane and Cadley Causeway to Woodplumpton Road. On Friday 6 May 1977 Ribble turned out dual-purpose Leyland Leopard No. 897 for the 18.00 dep. (18.25 ret.) to Redcar Avenue.

There were only three journeys each way on the P6. The 09.20 and 13.05 from Ingol and the 12.40 to Ingol were worked by Preston, while the 15.10 and 18.00 to Ingol and 18.25 return were worked by Ribble. MCCW-bodied Leyland PD3A/1 No. 70 was photographed at Lytham Road roundabout on 29 May 1978 working the 13.05 back from Ingol. This was the only route ever to be scheduled to run along Lytham Road to the Withy Trees.

From 3 November 1980 the P6 was designated as the 43 and all journeys were henceforth operated by Borough of Preston with OPO-equipped vehicles. The route continued to be technically jointly operated until 24 October 1986, and was the last remnant of the 1948 agreement. Seddon-bodied Leyland Panther No. 236 is also depicted at the Redcar Avenue terminus on 28 July 1981. There had never been a weekend service on the P6/43.

From 11 April 1988 the conventional 43 was withdrawn and replaced by a new service operated by minibuses. The new 43 ran via Brook Street, Eldon Street, Inkerman Street, Mill Lane, Cadley Causeway and Tag Lane and then looped around the Ingol estate with the terminus again being in Barry Avenue. It was the first service to use the north section of Inkerman Street since the Ashton B had been withdrawn in 1965 and it was the first service to be routed along Mill Lane. Northern Counties-bodied Dodge S56 No. 51 is seen in Inkerman Street on 3 February 1990. It ran for the last time on 21 October 2006.

Moor Nook

A service commenced running to what was then known as the Moorside district of Ribbleton on 10 July 1939. It terminated at the junction of Miller Road and Ullswater Road (since renamed Village Drive). The service was partially extended along Pope Lane from 30 August 1948 to Moor Nook Farm. From September 1950 the terminus was altered to Ribbleton Hall Drive, with peak-time buses ceasing to terminate at Ullswater Road in March 1953. Leyland-bodied TD5c No. 38 is seen on the Moor Nook stand in Birley Street, *c.* 1954. (MRC)

From 3 May 1965 outbound buses on the MN were rerouted to run via Acregate Lane to Miller Road to accommodate the wider PD3s. Between August 1953 and December 1968 the MN was linked with the BR service. The normal town centre stand for the MN, during the 1960s, was in Church Street outside Miller Arcade. Fairly new MCCW-bodied Leyland PD3A/1 No. 71 is seen, c. 1966, on a temporary stand in North Road (circumstances unknown), close to the Express Coach Station. (MRC)

The Moor Nook service was converted to OPO on Monday to Saturday on 3 December 1971 (Sunday from 5 September 1976). The longer Panthers were then having difficulty negotiating the right-angled junctions in Acregate Lane and consequently outbound buses were further rerouted, from January 1973, to continue to Blackpool Road. Additionally, buses turned at Moor Nook via Fairsnape Road and Thornley Road. Marshall-bodied Leyland Panther No. 213 is seen making the turn into Blackpool Road on 28 March 1977.

In November 1980 the route was designated as the 7 and then further renumbered to 8 from 21 October 1985. From 26 October 1986 inbound buses were also routed via Ribbleton Avenue/Lane. Minibuses were introduced from 13 July 1987 and the route was further altered to use Ribbleton Avenue direct to Ribbleton Hall Drive and then loop round the estate. The route around the estate was further altered on a number of occasions. Northern Counties-bodied Renault S56 No. 84 was photographed in Ribbleton Avenue, approaching Ribbleton Hall Drive, on 1 April 1989.

From 29 May 2001 the service was further altered on the estate to serve Grizedale Crescent, while from 14 June 2004 Ribbleton Hall Drive was again used in both directions, vice outbound via Farringdon Lane. Low-floor Optare Solos were introduced to the route from 13 October 2006 as shown by No. 79, recorded on 10 December 2007 and which is seen in more or less the same location as the previous picture.

After a brief period of operation by Stagecoach, between January 2009 and March 2010, service 8 has remained largely unaltered and operated by bigger buses under Rotala ownership, although Solos were reintroduced in 2020. One of the first buses to be repainted by Rotala, in silver and blue, was Scania ELC Esteem-bodied No. 30910, which is seen in Pope Lane on 20 January 2016, completing the loop around the estate. This vehicle was reregistered in 2020 before eventually being sold in May 2021.

An additional service to Moor Nook, numbered 9 and routed via New Hall Lane, Blackpool Road and Miller Road, was operated between October 1989 and May 2001. Always minibus operated, it saw the use of Dodge/Renault and then Metrorider types. New MCW Metrorider No. 10, still without blue relief, is seen approaching the bus station on 13 April 1995. Stagecoach reintroduced the service in October 2007, and it was still running in 2021.

Longsands

Services to Longsands have generally been linked with the Brookfield services. The original Gamull Lane FR service, which commenced on 15 April 1937, had a few journeys extended along Fulwood Row to Longsands Lane from 30 May 1938. Other than a change of route letter/number the service remained virtually unchanged for the remainder of its existence. ELC-bodied Atlantean No. 135 is seen at the terminus on 17 February 1980 with the 14.20 return to town. MCCW-bodied Leyland PD3/4 No. 14 is on a bus enthusiast's special tour.

There were never more than six return journeys on Monday to Saturday, with a maximum of three on a Sunday. The route was converted to OPO from 2 December 1968 with the other Brookfield services, but it was still common to see crewed buses throughout the 1970s. On Sunday 2 August 1981, ELC-bodied Atlantean No. 112 was rostered for the 14.00 departure to Longsands Lane and is seen climbing the rural country lane of Fulwood Row. A final route number change to 6 took place on 25 November 1985, with the last journey operating on Sunday 12 July 1987.

During the next few years the Longsands area was greatly transformed with new road and house building, including the construction of a new motorway junction on the M6 (Junction 31A). The west end of Longsands Lane gained a new service numbered 5, from 16 October 1989, which had previously run to Brookfield but was altered to loop via the newly constructed Eastway and Andertons Way. From 12 November 1990 the route was altered to run via Deepdale Road, vice Cromwell Road, and then further rerouted from 14 June 2004 to run via Sedgwick Street, St Paul's Road and St George's Road to Deepdale Road. It was largely replaced by the Orbit routes from 22 October 2006. MCW Metrorider No. 26 was photographed in a vastly transformed Longsands Lane on 13 May 1998.

For the next ten years Longsands was served by the Orbit routes. However, following their withdrawal after 2 April 2016, the Fulwood Row via Holme Slack service 14 was altered to serve Longsands. Service 14 journeys ran the full length of Longsands Lane to Fulwood Row while the 14A turned round at the Andertons Arms. Optare Solo No. 20831 is seen at the latter terminus on the first day of operation, 4 April 2016.

Services 14/A were withdrawn after 1 September 2018 and after a brief period of having no service at all a new service 15 was introduced to run to Longsands, via Deepdale Road, from 18 February 2019. From 4 November 2019 this service was greatly extended from Longsands, via Fulwood Asda, Wychnor, Nog Tow (Cottam) and Woodplumpton Village to Broughton. This was again short-lived, with the 15 being replaced by new service 49 from 20 July 2020. Optare Solo No. 20788 is seen in Lancaster Road on 14 March 2019.

The new service 49 was introduced on 20 July 2020 and followed the same route as the 15 as far as Fulwood Asda and then ran via Pittman Way, Eastway, Longfield and Broadwood Drive to terminate at the RPH. Streetlites returned to the Preston Bus fleet in September 2021 when four buses were transferred from Rotala's subsidiary company Diamond Bus Northwest. No. 20189 is seen alongside Moor Park in Sir Tom Finney Way on the 49 on 15 September 2021.

Larches

The service to Larches estate commenced running on 4 April 1955, when alternate buses on the Lea P1 were diverted into the new estate to terminate at Greaves Town Lane. Ribble provided just one bus for the integrated jointly operated Larches/Lea P1 service. As previously mentioned, the combined service ran to/from Frenchwood via the town centre. Other than changes to the town centre bus stands the route remained unaltered until 15 February 1965 when the Lea journeys were renumbered to P3 and diverted to run via Bray Street and Waterloo Road. MCCW-bodied Leyland PD2/10 No. 83 is seen on Fishergate Railway Bridge some time during the early 1960s. (MRC)

The P1 and P3 services were converted to OPO from 6 April 1970, initially using Leyland Panthers until the first Leyland Atlanteans joined the fleet in 1974/5. ELC-bodied Leyland Atlantean No. 111 is pursued along an icy Fylde Road by a Marshall-bodied Leyland Panther on the Ashton A service, on 27 January 1979.

The Larches route was given the service number 27 and separated from both the Frenchwood and Lea services, with the latter being substantially rerouted from 3 November 1980. The 27 was converted to minibus operation between 21 April and 30 May 1987. The first ever substantial alteration to the route took place on 1 July 1991 when the service was rerouted outbound via Leighton Street and Pedder Street, vice Wellfield Road. MCW Metrorider No. 35 is seen crossing Leighton Street Railway Bridge on 27 May 2004. The granite setts were removed shortly afterwards and relaid in Winckley Street.

Service 127 was a peak-time variant of the 27, which ran via the Larches route and then continued on to terminate at Lea. It operated from 1 February 1988 until 21 October 2006, at which time service 27 was also replaced by the new Orbit routes. From 14 June 2004 the route of the 27/127 was substantially altered to run through the docklands estate (Riversway) in place of service 30, which was withdrawn. On 7 July 2004 ELC-bodied Atlantean No. 177 was photographed in Navigation Way heading for Lea via Larches. The 127 was invariably worked by big buses that had to avoid the Leighton Street bridge.

With the introduction of the Orbit routes in October 2006 some long-standing connections were lost as the route network was substantially recast. One such connection was a service from Ashton to the railway station. This was corrected from 30 July 2007 when the 87 was introduced to follow the old route of the 27 via Ashton Lane Ends to Larches and then continue to Lea via Thorntrees Avenue and Hawthorn Crescent. This route was short-lived and was withdrawn after 17 May 2008. However, it was reintroduced by Stagecoach on 23 March 2009 but again only lasted until 5 June 2010, on which date Optare Solo No. 47758 was photographed at the junction of Pedder Street and Ashton Street. Apart from the Ashton B and the 13, only outbound buses had been routed this way.

The 87 was then replaced by county council-supported service 77, which was operated by Stagecoach and worked through to Blackpool. The 89 was first introduced as part of the Orbit group, running mainly at peak times. From 22 March 2009 an enhanced service was provided to run additionally via Thorntrees Avenue and Hawthorn Crescent. Monday 21 May 2012 saw the route again altered to start in Lune Street and, other than peak-time journeys, operate only as far as Larches. It moved back to the bus station on 3 September 2012 and a week later became the full Sunday variant of the Orbit routes to the west of the city. From 4 April 2016 a new 89 variant commenced that served both Riversway and Thorntrees Avenue. Shortly afterwards it was altered to serve the Port Way Park & Ride site. From 3 September 2018 it was curtailed to terminate at Larches at all times. Scania Omnidekka No. 40406 is seen in Lancaster Road on 29 August 2019. The 89 was linked with the 16 and renumbered to 100, in recognition of the centenary, in July 2021.

Lea

As previously recounted, the P1 was a jointly operated service from Frenchwood to Lea, which replaced both the Ashton Lane Ends D and the Frenchwood FR from 1 January 1948. It was extended to Aldfield Avenue from 4 April 1955. This early 1960s view depicts Crossley-bodied Leyland PD2/10 No. 23 in Blackpool Road, passing the previous Lea terminus of Victoria Park Drive (on the right beyond the restaurant).

Other than the extension at Lea the route remained virtually unchanged until 13 February 1965 when it was altered to run via Bray Street and Waterloo Road (replacing the Ashton B) and renumbered to P3. It remained fully interworked with the P1. The P1/P3 were converted to OPO on 6 April 1970 and Marshall-bodied Leyland Panther No. 215 is seen in Waterloo Road on 12 October 1980. This road is no longer served by a bus route.

From 3 November 1980 the P3 was renumbered to 26. The main route was substantially altered to run via North Road, Garstang Road and Blackpool Road before continuing on to Lea. However, some peak-time journeys continued to run via the old route using the same service number. Latterly reduced to a single inbound journey via Waterloo Road, the service number 26 to Lea didn't finally disappear until the late 1990s. Marshall-bodied Leyland Panther No. 216 is seen in North Road on 25 March 1981.

Both services 24 (Ashton) and 26 (Lea) were withdrawn on 25 June 1984 and replaced by new service 25, which followed the former's route to Ashton (Pedders Lane) and then continued on to Lea. It then continued to operate as such for the next twenty years when, from 14 June 2004, it was replaced on a Sunday by service 127. Guild-92 Advertising bus Leyland Olympian No. 35 was photographed at the Lea terminus in Aldfield Avenue on 19 May 1991.

Service 24 ran as per the 25 but also served Thorntrees Avenue and Hawthorn Crescent. It commenced on 5 December 1988 and initially ran to an infrequent timetable using minibuses. From 16 October 1989 it was integrated into the 25 timetable and was henceforth operated by big buses. There then followed several alterations to both the 24 and 25 services that affected the type of vehicle used and the days and times of operation, before the services were finally withdrawn by Stagecoach after 21 March 2009. The majority of the 25 route was then served by Stagecoach service 68, which was still the case in 2021. Former Lothian Buses Leyland Olympian No. 132 is seen emerging from Campion Drive on 11 May 2005.

Preston Bus reintroduced a service to Lea from 7 October 2010 by extending the 31 from Savick. The daytime service was withdrawn from 21 May 2012 and replaced by the 31A, which also served Thorntrees Avenue and Hawthorn Crescent. The 31/31A continued to run until 2 April 2016 when the latter was withdrawn and the former altered to terminate at Savick. From 4 April 2016, on which date Optare Solo No. 20791 was photographed in Port Way, service 89 was introduced running to Lea on a daily basis.

Between 4 April 2016 and 2 September 2018, the 31 turned round by looping around the Savick estate, after which it was again extended via Blackpool Road, Thorntrees Avenue and Hawthorn Crescent to terminate at Lea Aldfield Avenue; at the same time the 89 was curtailed at Larches. Optare Solo SR No. 20701, having been displaced from the Walton-le-Dale Park & Ride service, was about to turn out of Cottam Lane into Blackpool Road when photographed on 9 January 2019.

Savick

The P7 to Savick commenced running on 14 October 1974 and was routed via Ashton Lane Ends and West Park Avenue and then around the estate to the terminus in Luton Road. Initial operation was with crewed double-deckers, but it was converted to OPO using Bristol LHS minibuses from 30 August 1976. Having been renumbered to 30 in November 1980, the Bristols continued until 25 October 1986 when the route reverted to operation with big buses and diverted to terminate at a new turning circle in Savick Way. Minibuses were reintroduced from 21 April 1987 and various significant alterations to the route followed, including running via docklands. The 30 variant of the Savick routes ran for the last time on 13 June 2004. Duple-bodied Bristol LHS No. 342 is seen in Birkdale Drive on 7 February 1981.

Service 31 to Savick commenced running on 16 October 1989 and was routed via Brook Street, being fully interworked with service 30. There were many alterations over the following thirty years, including periods of operation through to Lea, which was the case in 2021. MCW Metrorider No. 36 is seen in Savick Way, where it is making a double-run to the turning circle and back following its trip around the estate. Number 36 is seen on its first day in service – 7 April 1998.

MCW Metrorider No. 1 is seen in Lea Road on 14 May 2004. Service 29 to Savick was routed via Fishergate Hill and Strand Road (the only service ever to be routed via West Strand other than Works buses) and then through the docklands estate, etc., to West Park Avenue. It operated at Monday to Friday peak times only, between 28 January 1991 and 11 June 2004.

One of the oddest routes to have been operated was the Inner Link 13. Conceived by the council's Transport Committee, it was intended as a Christmas shopper's service and ran on Saturdays only between 9 October 1982 and 15 January 1983. The route could be classed as an inner circle, and it traversed a number of streets that had never had a bus route before or since. Requiring just the one bus and running in a clockwise direction only, it was always worked by one of the Bristol LHS minibus types. No. 342 is seen at the timing point in Pedder Street on the last Saturday of operation.

Tanterton

The newly built Tanterton estate gained its first bus service on 3 November 1980 when the Ashton C was extended from Lane Ends using the service number 33. Early mornings, evenings and Sunday journeys were interworked with the 44 (Ingol), which from 14 June 2004 fully replaced the 33 at these times. From 13 July 1987 inbound buses were altered to run via Plungington Road and Adelphi Street. From January 1991 it was one of a number of services that were altered to use Ring Way outbound following the closure of the Friargate bus lane. ELC-bodied Leyland Atlantean No. 153 is seen heading south along Tag Lane working back to town on 18 July 1981.

Eighteen Dennis Tridents with ELC's attractive Lolyne bodies were purchased in 1999/2000. Seven were dedicated to the 33/35 services and seven were dedicate to the 22/23 services, all with appropriate route branding. The remaining four didn't carry any branding. They were introduced to services 33/35 from 13 December 1999, with the 35 having commenced running to Tanterton via Fylde Road from 16 October 1989. No. 190 is seen in lower Friargate on 7 April 2000. Route branding was removed in 2007, although the buses continued in service until 2018/9, latterly mainly on school services.

It was intended that new ELC Esteem Scanias would take over on the 35 from 28 July 2007, upon withdrawal of service 33, but ELC was somewhat behind with their orders. The last of the Atlanteans were also withdrawn at this time and Preston Bus was short of buses. Consequently, an arrangement was made whereby a number of buses were taken on loan in lieu of the delayed Esteems. Volvo's Wright-bodied B7RLE BXO7 AZJ, carrying Preston Bus fleetnames and the number 235, is seen picking up in Lancaster Road on 15 August 2007.

A scene recorded at the bus station during the brief period of Stagecoach ownership, on 26 March 2009. Stagecoach moved the low-floor, single-deck buses to services 19/22 and put mainly Tridents back on the 35. However, in this instance Olympian No. 14556 has been allocated to the route. Following resumption of the service by Preston Bus on 15 March 2010 the route continued to be mainly operated by Tridents. Between April 2016 and January 2019, the 35 was one of a handful of services to offer late-night departures.

As the Tridents were retired from front-line duty, single-deck types took over most duties on the 35. The route has remained unaltered since its inception in October 1989 except for a minor deviation on Sundays via the Ingol estate between October 2007 and June 2010. Mercedes Citaro No. 33006 is seen in Tulketh Brow, at Ashton Lane Ends, on 15 February 2019. The Ashton Lane Ends C used to depart from behind the new health centre, although back in the day it was a petrol filling station that occupied that plot.

From 13 June 1983 Tanterton was served by another route when the 28 was extended from the Lightfoot Lane terminus via Lightfoot Lane to Nog Tow and then to loop via Tag Lane and Tanterton Hall Road. Alexander-bodied Leyland Atlantean No. 110 is seen in Lightfoot Lane returning to town on 18 June 1983. It is passing the junction of Wychnor with Preston Grasshoppers rugby ground situated behind the hedge on the right.

From 13 July 1987 the service number was changed to 32, although the number 28 remained vacant until October 1998. Modified Alexander-bodied Atlantean No. 143 is seen on the western section of Lightfoot Lane, near Nog Tow, working back to the bus station on 9 August 1995. This section of Lightfoot Lane is now a cul-de-sac while No. 143 was one of the last two Atlanteans in service, not being withdrawn until 29 August 2007.

From 27 October 1997 the route was converted to operation with minibuses and ran in conjunction with new service 36, which ran beyond Tanterton to Cottam. From 12 February 2001 the route was altered at Cottam to loop via Merry Trees Lane and Cottam Way. From 14 June 2004 service 32 was dropped with all journeys running as the 36, which was altered to return via the east side of Tanterton Hall Road, vice Tom Benson Way. Following the introduction of the Orbit routes on 22 October 2006, the route was altered to terminate at Tanterton and subsequently withdrawn entirely (other than the 136 school journey) after 28 July 2007. MCW Metrorider No. 29 is seen at the Tanterton terminus on 21 July 2007.

Many months of planning were undertaken before the route of the Orbit services was finalised. The route was in excess of 17 miles long and provided a connection between a number of districts and the city centre. Contributions to the operating costs were made by both the city and county councils. Eleven new Optare Solos were purchased specifically for the route, this being the number of vehicles initially required to operate the schedule. In the picture above Optare Solo No. 20790 is seen crossing the Lancaster Canal in Lea Road on 29 October 2014 on the anticlockwise circuit, while below Wrightbus Streetlite No. 20909 is seen in St Paul's Road on 11 July 2013 on the clockwise circuit. The services commenced on 22 October 2006 running every fifteen minutes on Monday to Saturday, with a reduced timetable on Sunday. The weekday frequency was subsequently reduced to every twenty minutes and the Sunday schedule was withdrawn and replaced by services 86 and 89. The service was withdrawn in its entirety after 2 April 2016; the reason cited was excessive operating costs. A somewhat skeleton 88 service, running hourly on Monday to Friday between the RPH and Larches via Ingol and Cottam has been provided since the cessation of the Orbit routes.

Following the implementation of deregulation in October 1986, the initial concern was from competition to bus services within the town boundaries, which provoked a tit-for-tat battle with newcomers Zippy (United Transport). This was a real concern throughout 1987/8. However, Preston Bus themselves were not shy in introducing new services, which took their buses to places they had never been to before. Service 39 was an ambitious service that operated to Blackpool and ran between July and September 1988. Alexander-bodied Atlanteans from the batch of Nos 141–50 were used during the week, while minibuses provided the service on a Sunday. Number 143 is seen leaving Talbot Road bus station in Blackpool on 18 July 1988.

Another more local service was the 4, which commenced running to Penwortham on 16 May 1988. It was normally worked by minibuses but some peak-time journeys produced bigger buses, as evidenced by ELC-bodied Leyland Atlantean No. 158, which was recorded in Fishergate on 12 July 1989. Further services to Longton (3) and Bamber Bridge (17) were also introduced, but all three were withdrawn by October 1989 following an agreement with Ribble (who had since acquired Zippy) to rationalise services.

Between 9 November 1987 and 13 October 1989 service 31 was provided running during the day on Monday to Friday. It ran direct from the bus station via the A6 to Broughton then did a one-way loop via Woodplumpton and Nog Tow back to Garstang Road. Somewhat strangely, considering the country roads it traversed, it was operated by Atlanteans. ELC-bodied No. 111 is seen in Tabley Lane, approaching Nog Tow, on 17 February 1989. The service number 31 was immediately reused for a new service to Savick (see page 77).

Service changes then remained fairly local for the next twenty years before stability was again threaten by competition. In June 2007 Stagecoach commenced a very aggressive expansion policy of their services in the city, which eventually led to the acquisition of Preston Bus in January 2009. Retaliation by Preston Bus during this period was more of a token gesture rather than an all-guns-blazing reply. Service 2 was introduced running to Southport on 9 July 2007 in competition to Stagecoach's similar route. Leyland Olympian No. 108, deputising for a Lynx, is seen in Lancaster Road, at the start of its journey, on 21 August 2007. The route ceased to operate after 3 May 2008.

Service 68 ran from Preston to Blackpool via Lytham and St Annes and was actually part of Stagecoach's route network. However, in 2010, Stagecoach withdrew their Sunday to Thursday evening service. The re-established Preston Bus gained the contract from the county council to operate the journeys that had been withdrawn by Stagecoach. The times of departure of these workings made it somewhat difficult to photograph, but nevertheless Optare Solo No. 20790 was caught on camera at Lytham Square at around 8 p.m. on 4 June 2013. This arrangement came to an end after 3 April 2016 when Stagecoach reintroduced some late evening journeys on those days of the week.

A similar situation arose when Stagecoach withdrew their evening departures on their 113 service, which ran from Preston to Wigan via Bamber Bridge, Lostock Hall, Eccleston and Wrightington. Preston Bus was awarded the contract to provide the evening service from 31 October 2011. Optare Solo No. 20795 was photographed at Heskin with a return evening journey to Preston on 24 July 2014. This route also passed back to Stagecoach at the beginning of April 2016.

In September 2014 both Preston Bus and Transdev Burnley entered into an agreement with Myerscough College to provide a network of bus services to transport students to the college in the morning and take them home again in the evening. The services operated by Preston Bus were the 400 (Fleetwood), 401 (local shuttle), 433 (Preston Railway Station), 437 (Preston Bus Station), 853 (St Annes), and 995 (Clitheroe), while Transdev provided the buses for the 852 (Burnley). All of these services were still running in 2021. Optare Solo No. 20795 is seen again in the college grounds on 29 September 2014 on the local shuttle service to nearby Bilsborough (A6).

The original service 12 to Longton had previously operated as the 3B, but was introduced as the 12 from 23 July 2012 with a different routing; there was also a 12A, which also served Broadgate. From 4 April 2016 the 12A was dropped and the 12 was altered to start from Lune Street. There has been minor tweaking to the route since, including a back projection to the bus station in August 2021. This autumnal setting sees Optare Solo No. 20785 just setting back from Longton on 27 October 2016.

Preston Bus first branched out into the Fylde (other than the 68) on 9 December 2013 when service 75 (Blackpool) and 75A (Newton-with-Scales), both running from Preston, were won on tender from the county council. Over the next seven years a variety of services, which changed a number of times, were operated. These included the 74 (two versions), 75 (three versions), 75A (four versions), 76, 77, 77A and 80. The various routes took Preston Buses all over Fylde, even as far away as Fleetwood, and at the height of operations, in 2016–18, five Optare Solos were outstationed at premises in Blackpool. Optare Solo No. 20773 is seen climbing Preston Street in Kirkham on 21 April 2018 while working back from Fleetwood to Preston on the final version of the 75.

Service 76 didn't originate from Preston and ran from Lytham St Annes to Blackpool via Kirkham, Great Eccleston and Singleton. The two buses required for this service operated out of the Blackpool outstation. Long term loanee from Diamond Bus Northwest, Optare Solo No. 20802, is seen nearing journey's end at Lytham on 3 April 2018. The service was operated from 11 December 2017 to 16 February 2019.

Service 80 ran from Preston to Myerscough College via Catforth, Elswick and Great Eccleston. Preston Bus was awarded the county council contract to operate the service from 14 April 2014. From 4 April 2016 the route out of the city was substantially altered to serve the railway station, vice Friargate. Optare Solo No. 20778 is seen in the picturesque village of Great Eccleston on the first day of operation; it was replaced by the 77A from 11 December 2017. The last Fylde services were relinquished on 19 July 2020.

One of the most interesting services ever operated by any Preston bus was the 37-mile-long 280, and its X80 and 180 variants, which ran from Preston to Skipton via Clitheroe. The origin of the route stretched way back to when Ribble Motors first operated its X27 service, which connected Skipton and Liverpool via Preston. Preston Bus took over the partially supported service from 4 April 2016. It was normally operated by single deck types but on Sunday 17 July 2016 Volvo B9TL No. 40628, which was recorded in the centre of Whalley, was one of three of the type allocated to the route on that day. Alas the operator withdrew from the route on 15 June 2019 with operation passing to Stagecoach the following day.

Preston Bus won the county council contract to operate a number of services based on Clitheroe, commencing on 11 December 2017. These initially comprised service 2 (Clitheroe town service), 3 (Sawley), 5 (Chipping), 25/A (Blackburn/Mellor) and 35 (Blackburn to Longridge). Five Optare Solos were required to operate the group of routes, although these were replaced by five brand new Mellor-bodied Mercedes Sprinter minibuses, branded as the Ribble Valley Network, from July 2018. The 25A (Blackburn to Mellor Brook) was withdrawn after 17 February 2018 as was service 35 after 2 November 2019. The latter was then replaced by new service 45, which ran from Preston to Blackburn via Broughton, Goosnargh, Longridge and the previous 35 route. *Above*: Mercedes Sprinter No. 21200 has paused briefly at Mellor on 25 July 2018 on service 25 (Blackburn to Clitheroe). *Below*: Operation of all these services, except the reinstated 25A on a Sunday and the 45, passed to other operators after 18 July 2020. Optare Solo No. 20776 is seen in the centre of Chipping on service 5 on the penultimate day of operation. Four of the Sprinters were subsequently transferred to Diamond Bus Northwest.

As previously mentioned, service 45, which ran from Preston to Blackburn, was a replacement for the 35. Operated by Optare Solos, it commenced on 4 November 2019. Following the loss of the Ribble Valley Network services, the 45 was retained and joined by new service 46, which ran from Preston to Longridge via Garstang Road, Mill Lane, Ingol, Nog Tow, Woodplumpton, Broughton and Goosnargh. It was a part replacement for the 15 from Nog Tow to Broughton and interworked with the 45 between Broughton and Longridge. Optare Solo No. 20790 is seen in the village of Goosnargh on 30 July 2020.

Another group of routes operated by Preston Bus, from 4 April 2016, comprised the 3A, which ran from Burscough to Appley Bridge via Skelmersdale and the Ormskirk local town services 5 and 6. From 24 July 2017 the 3A was replaced by two new routes, the 312 Skelmersdale to Wrightington and the 313 Skelmersdale to Burscough. Initially operated by Optare Solos, three more Mercedes Sprinter minibuses were obtained in June 2019 to work the 312/3 services. Mellor-bodied Mercedes Sprinter No. 21231 was photographed at Parbold on 18 June 2019 working a 313 service duty to Skelmersdale.

Two further services in West Lancashire were gained on tender commencing on 11 December 2017. These were the 337 from Chorley to Ormskirk via Eccleston, Mawdesley, Parbold and Burscough and the 347 from Chorley to Southport via Eccleston, Croston, Rufford and Banks. Optare Solo SR No. 20875 was one of five of the type, which had previously seen service on the island of Malta, which were acquired by Preston Bus in January 2018. It is seen in Lord Street in Southport working the 347 to Chorley on 9 May 2018.

Preston Bus first became involved with Park & Ride in November 1988 with a Christmas service from Adelphi Street to the town centre. A more permanent service was the operation of the Port Way service, from Lune Street, which was taken over from Stagecoach on 28 January 1991. This ran until 21 May 2016, latterly connected to the Walton-le-Dale service, when it was superseded by service 89. From 1 December 2002 Preston Bus also operated the Walton service until it was taken over by Stagecoach after 6 July 2019. Three new Optare Versas were dedicated to the service in January 2012 and No. 30124 is seen in Lancaster Road on 6 June 2012. A number of other such services have been operated over the years, generally in connection with short-term events.

Baths Specials first began running in 1938, three years after Saul Street Baths was opened. Saul Street closed in 1991 and thereafter primary school pupils were transported to either Fulwood or West View Leisure Centres for their swimming lessons. Preston Bus finally relinquished the 'Baths' contract in 2015. As many as four buses could be employed at the same time as evidenced by PD3s Nos 2, 15 and 59 and Atlantean No. 114, which are seen waiting in Lancaster Road on 9 February 1978.

Football Specials have been operated since at least the second decade of the twentieth century when trams used to be lined up opposite the stadium in Deepdale Road. Just prior to the Second World War a network of specials from a number of the town's districts commenced running. These were reinstated after the war, with upwards of twenty buses being employed on match days throughout the 1950s and early 1960s. Gradually these dwindled but two dedicated services were still being run at the start of the 2021/22 season. Olympian No. 42558 has just arrived at the ground with the service from Cottam and Tanterton on 15 September 2012 for the match against Crawley Town.

The first recorded school bus service was from Pedders Lane to the 'Modern Schools', which commenced on 29 August 1929. Since then the operator has been heavily involved in the transportation of scholars to the present day. Preston College (formerly W. R. Tuson College), Corpus Christie and Archbishop Temple schools, all of which are situated in St Vincent's Road, are among the schools that have been served over the years. This array of buses comprising Leyland PD3/4 No. 16, Atlantean No. 120 and PD3A/1s Nos 87, 69, 90 and 84 are seen waiting in the St Vincent's Road bus compound for school's out on 30 September 1976. Five school services were still provided to Corpus Christie in 2021.

A number of dedicated hospital services have also been provided over the years, most notably to Sharoe Green and the Continuation hospitals. The latter was first served from 16 December 1951 by diverting a handful of journeys on the Fulwood Row FR service. From 17 May 1954 a dedicated service was provided that ran on certain days and at certain times. Seddon-bodied Leyland Panther No. 231 is seen cautiously making its way along Fulwood Hall Lane with the 14.15 departure to the hospital on Sunday 27 January 1979. The service ran for the last time on 1 June 1984, following the closure of the hospital. Also of note was the infrequent service 99, which ran from Moor Nook to RPH between March 1981 and July 2007.

On 11 December 1964 the Corporation commenced running a sponsored Free Shoppers' service from Lancaster Road to Allways Store (later renamed Fame and then Asda), which was situated in an old mill in Dundonald Street at Fishwick. The service was worked by one of the two Leyland PS1s until they were withdrawn in December 1968; thereafter a PD3 was provided (no conductor was required). MCCW-bodied Leyland PD3/4 No. 14 is seen outside the store on 2 October 1977, a year before the store closed. A network of Free Shoppers' services, which required three Atlanteans, was subsequently operated to/from the Fulwood Asda store between August 1986 and December 1990.

For the summer season in 2017–19 Preston Bus operated the 830 service on Sundays and bank holidays. This ran from Preston to Richmond and was part of the bus/rail leisure network marketed as Dalesbus. There was also an add-on journey to Leyburn. The duty was generally undertaken by a Wrightbus Streetlite and more often than not in its final year by No. 32306. In this view the bus has arrived at Ribblehead and is about to negotiate a short track on the left, which leads up to the station yard where it will pick up passengers from a Carlisle to Leeds train. This view was recorded on 22 June 2019.

Over a long period of time Preston buses have occasionally been called upon to operate rail-replacement services; most recently during the prolonged period of electrification works that were undertaken on the Preston to Manchester line. However, this picture depicts ELC-bodied Leyland Atlanteans Nos 165 and 167, which are standing on a splendid array of granite setts, in front of the old East Lancashire side of Preston station. The date is 28 April 1984 and they were two of eight Preston buses that were substituting for trains on the Blackpool line. Everything on view has since been swept away in the name of progress.

In the past numerous works services have been provided over the years. These were mainly to the mills or the large Strand Road engineering complex. During the 1950s/1960s significant numbers of Preston double-deckers, along with buses from other operators, would be waiting for the factory hooter to sound at Dick, Kerr's/English Electric, which signalled the exodus home. A number of buses also ran at lunchtime. MCCW-bodied Leyland PD3A/1 No. 90 is setting out back to town on 5 January 1980, following the end of the Saturday morning shift. The last such works buses ceased to operate sometime during the final decade of the twentieth century.